BECOMING A FINANCIAL CRITICAL THINKER
COPYRIGHT © 2023 Bergen Brown Jr.

Published by WWM Financial Literacy LLC

ISBN   979-8-9877027-0-3   ebook
         979-8-9877027-1-0   paperback
         979-8-9877027-2-7   hardcover

Library of Congress Control Number: 2023901389

First Edition
Book Production and Publishing by Brands Through Books
brandsthroughbooks.com

myfinancialwalk.com

5-STEP PROCESS
FOR BULLETPROOF FINANCES

BECOMING A
FINANCIAL
CRITICAL THINKER

BERGEN BROWN JR.

WWM FINANCIAL LITERACY LLC

CONTENTS

NOTE TO READERS

This book contains the opinions and ideas of its author. It is intended to provide helpful and informative material on the subjects addressed. The strategies outlined in this book may not be suitable for every individual and are not guaranteed or warranted to provide any particular results.

This book is sold with the understanding that neither the author nor the publisher is engaged in rendering legal, financial, accounting, or other professional advice or services. The reader should consult a competent professional before adopting any of the suggestions in this book or drawing inferences from it.

No warranty is made with respect to the accuracy or completeness of the information or referenced contained herein, and both the author and the publisher specifically disclaim any responsibility for any liability, loss, or risk, personal or otherwise, which is incurred as a consequence, directly or indirectly, of the use and application of any of the contents of this book.

INTRODUCTION

Financial literacy is a term that people often hear but do not fully understand. They crave to understand it because money management skills have the potential to unlock financial freedom. But desperation to learn about money makes people the target of misunderstanding. Apparently, by the looks of the internet, everybody is an overnight expert. Have you ever heard, "Let me show you how I turned $100 into $100,000 in six months" or "Let me repair your credit?" Well, guess how many people successfully turned $100 into $100,000?

Zero.

And guess how many people fixed their spending habits by fixing their credit?

Zero.

There's no way around the fact that you need to educate yourself to find success managing money. You can't take the elevator straight to the top. Instead, you must take the stairs, one by one. In other words, rely on progressively working toward your financial goals instead of executing them all at once. Don't continue searching for a way down easy street. When you quickly acquire money, be sure not to dispose of it even faster. Mindset is one piece of financial literacy that folks tend to overlook, but your mindset is the most important factor when understanding personal finances. Many are in denial that they have a problem with overspending or need help. However, a closed mind won't open new doors nor turn over a new leaf.

TODAY IS A NEW DAY!

From this day forward, you will no longer accept financial advice from your uncle who doesn't know the first thing about a budget. I've wasted too many years taking generic advice from people with no clue how money works. Did you know that a higher income has a stronger correlation with education (degree level) and experience than financial literacy? Anyone can become a high-income earner if they learn to solve other people's problems. I know guys that make hundreds of thousands and spend hundreds of thousands on worthless items. Besides the designer clothes and luxury, leased cars, some are just as broke as everyone else, although their material possessions lead people to believe otherwise.

WHAT ABOUT THE "GURUS?"

I've read just about every book by famous financial authors with a significant influence on everyday people. They give useful information, but each has a different method to their madness (financial philosophy). One author teaches to use debt to create cash flow, and another guru tells their readers to stay debt-free and that all debt is bad debt. Finally, there's that guy who tells you, "It's as easy as one, two, three, with none of your own money involved!"

And guess whom everyone gravitates toward?

The guy who claims he can show you how to put money in your pocket today.

People believe that if they increase their income, all their problems will disappear.

PLEASE UNDERSTAND

Income is one of many subjects of personal finance that people allow to consume their focus. Nearly all lottery winners are back to square one after a short time.

Why?

Because receiving a lot of money doesn't equate to making sound financial decisions. When people get some money, they often buy everything they want and save the remaining money (if anything is left). When they can't rely on the amount of money they have, they borrow money from other sources, which is called debt. On all social class levels, credit is used irresponsibly.

Why?

Because most folks don't effectively manage their money and instead search for other sources to continue their unaffordable lifestyle.

WALK WITH ME

I understand numbers aren't for everybody, but every adult should sit down and make critical financial decisions regarding their hard-earned money. Did you know that most Americans can't afford a $1,000 emergency (Brooks 2023)? If that doesn't bother you, maybe you never had to struggle or don't know anyone fighting to survive. I know too many people that are struggling. In fact, I know how it feels to struggle.

Seventeen years ago, during a freezing winter, my family and I shared a couch and huddled under my sister's comforter. We didn't have any heat, and we could see our breath when we talked. Everyone was so cold that we would argue about who should change the DVD when a movie ended because nobody wanted to get up from under the covers. That winter, my mother worked her butt off to put things under our Christmas tree, only for those items to be stolen weeks before Christmas. As a child, I felt stressed (with no obligation) to provide for my family. I cannot imagine the financial stress my mother carried during those times. I was sick of it, and I was sick of feeling helpless and trapped.

In the last decade, during my free time, I've dedicated my life to studying personal finance and accounting. Accounting is the language of business, which ultimately helped me to read numbers. Along my journey, I've shared my knowledge with family, friends, and social media, and I'll piece together the puzzle for you. When you finish reading this book, managing money will make sense. This will be the most thorough but straightforward way to view personal finance. You will be capable of making critical financial decisions in your household. As you turn each page, be ready to turn a new leaf. Refuse to quit. You owe it to yourself.

Everything you've learned in life has a fundamental approach. For every subject, there's a fundamental baseline to solve equations. In America, we're free, but there are laws we must follow. Well, I'm going to let you in on a little secret: we learn basic skills as children for how to treat people, otherwise known as golden rules. These rules are in place because we tend to have better outcomes when following rules. However, you can run the risk of avoiding the rules and getting the equation wrong in the classroom, end up in jail for not following the law, or find yourself in a street brawl for disrespecting someone's grandmother. In each scenario, you have a greater chance of receiving a better outcome by following the fundamentals.

HOW ABOUT SPORTS?

Most people know someone with a natural-born talent in sports. The entire neighborhood just knew that person would make it to the pros. Over the years, that child depended on their talent, never training in their spare time and rarely accepting advice. Eventually, that kid was no longer better than everyone else because other kids worked harder on their fundamentals.

Let's tie that example to the San Antonio Spurs Hall of Famer Tim Duncan. Tim is arguably the most boring but fundamentally sound NBA player the world has ever seen. What's so remarkable is that Duncan didn't learn to play basketball until he was a teenager, only to stun the world with such high achievements by sticking to the fundamentals. Tim quietly won NBA Rookie of the Year, two NBA MVP Awards, five NBA championships, and three NBA Finals MVP Awards. His style of play showed the world that anyone could achieve high levels of success if they stuck to the basics.

Tim's story is my way of encouraging you to understand the fundamentals before making a significant financial decision, such as buying a house you can't afford to furnish. That house will be yours in due time, but for now, stick to the basics. As my mom would say, "Build a house on a solid foundation. That way, no storms can destroy what you build." The foundation of a house is made to last forever. If you plan to build a legacy on a solid foundation, let's walk.

I need you to take a good look at the illustration below. This is the foundation of the fundamentals of personal finance in chronological order from top to bottom.

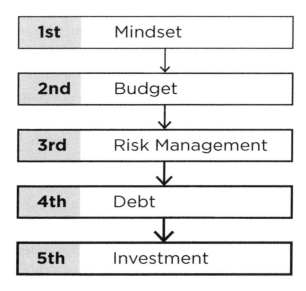

THE STRUCTURE OF PERFECT FINANCES

Each person is unique—the way you see the world may differ from my perspective. Our salaries differ. Some of us have more medical needs than others. The cost of living is different in every neighborhood. The list of differences goes on. Everyone faces challenges, but most challenges have a unique root associated with money. The picture above is a five-step bulletproof system to achieve a solid financial life. This system is entirely do-it-yourself and will potentially increase your income, reduce your debt, and create more buying power in your life.

Walk with me to learn more about the five-step system.

Step One: Mindset—Get Your Mind Right. Life's challenges require you to make critical decisions that positively or negatively impact your world. The outcome depends on your decision-making skills. This requires you to be a critical thinker, starting with your mindset. If you want to win in life, you must first win within yourself. Mentally pull yourself out of the hole you dug and get on your feet. You will be dirty, sweaty, and exhausted, but you can clean yourself off after putting in the work. Never forget that you are your biggest investment.

Step Two: Budget—Run It Up With a Strategy. Creating a budget is the first place to start when changing the dynamics of your family tree. A budget is the most underrated and underutilized yet valuable tool. Everything you pay for should come from your budget. Everything you invest in should come from your budget. When creating a budget, you will find out if you have an income problem or a spending problem. A budget provides structure, also known as financial stability. A budget allows you to prioritize what's important in the most efficient way. Creating a budget also involves exploring the topic that most people want to discuss: "How do I make money?"
Well, let's talk about it.

Step Three: Risk Management—Secure the Bag and Protect Yo' Neck. Once you structure your money with a bulletproof budget, you must minimize your risk exposure. The more assets you acquire, the more you have to lose. Protect what you own. That means acquiring insurance is mandatory. While you build up that rainy day fund, don't lose it or any other assets you own to something that could have been avoided. Remember, it's not about what you can make; it's about what you can keep. You have to pay the cost to be the boss.

Step Four: Debt Management—Build Financial Trust. Why do employers, businesses, and lenders check your credit score when you make an inquiry? I'll tell you: your credit score tells someone how trustworthy you are, and that's precisely how you need to view the topic. Trust is built over time, not overnight. When you break someone's trust, it takes time to restore it, and the same goes for your credit. Put yourself in the shoes of an entrepreneur looking for a business partner. They probably want to work with an honest, responsible person, right? So, would they partner with someone with poor credit looking for the easiest way to wipe away their financial responsibilities or a person who owns their mistakes and corrects them? The answer is obvious. Bottom line: Pay what you owe and find value in your lessons.

Step Five: Investment—We Love Looking Into the Crystal Ball. Whenever people decide to get their lives together, they start on the last step: investments. Everyone falls victim here. People want to make money and dive head-first into the deep end. The only way to create multiple streams of income is by leveraging your time. Long-term investments will make you a lot of money over time, but I'm going to help you understand how to invest with minimal risk and maximize your most valuable asset: time.

WARNING: My five-step system may be defective to anyone that bends the rules. You cannot invest without a solid budget. Be smart. Don't gamble with your life.

Let's walk.

List three lessons you want to learn about money management.

1. ....

2. ....

3. ....

Why is it important to learn those topics? (Your motives might include family, loss, change, struggle, bad decisions, etc.)

....

....

....

Do you understand that you are responsible for the change from this moment forward? Circle *yes* or *no*.

If yes, let's walk.

PART I

MINDSET

UNLEARN AND RELEARN

Let me start by saying that I didn't always have life figured out.

I've always aspired to be a businessman (whatever that means), and my friends had similar dreams. They say, "Birds of a feather flock together," right? Well, I was one of the last to fly free from the flock. The others were handed prison sentences of at least ten years. My life involved struggle after struggle, and my depression increased by the day. It wasn't looking good for me at all. I could feel in the air that the end was near. After being the victim of six robberies and the experiences of living in poverty without my father's guidance, I believed it was my time to check out. I remember walking into the credit union, asking the clerk how to invest, and making sure my investment went to my younger brother if anything happened to me. She led me to a certificate of deposit (CD) and two different US bonds, of which I made him the co-owner. Not long after that, I received a call that my sister's boyfriend was killed by gun violence, and someone needed to pick her up off the emergency room floor.

My sister took his loss extremely hard and informed us that she was pregnant. From that moment on, I found purpose in life. I didn't want my nephew to grow up without a father figure or someone to look up to and admire. So, I walked into the Marine's office (Army and Air Force) to leave my current environment and start over. After being denied by those service branches, I walked out of the recruitment building and was stopped by a gentleman in a blue uniform. We exchanged words, and I told him I needed to leave as soon as possible. In about one month, he had me on my way to boot camp.

At that point, according to the military, everything I'd learned in life was wrong. I had to unlearn and relearn everything, from how I tied my shoes to how I spoke. Most importantly, I chose to accept those changes. However, I was still depressed. My sister was dealing with the most challenging obstacle of her life, grieving while pregnant. My younger brother was left to fend for himself in a crime-infested neighborhood. My lovely mother had nothing but faith left to her name. Growing up as the man of the house from the age of nine until adulthood due to my father's lengthy prison sentence, I made it my responsibility to protect and guide my family. My mind wouldn't let me excuse the fact that I was doing a crappy job because everyone around me was struggling.

Eventually, when I was further into my military career, I had surgery and nearly flatlined. My doctors were impressed with how I handled the surgical procedure, but I didn't care. Life had run its course for me. There wasn't much more I cared to see.

The following year, my ship pulled into New York City for Fleet Week. I met a woman at a bar that showed interest in my job, and she gave me an offer—if I showed her my job on the ship, she would show me her job in the city. The next day, she arrived at my ship as promised, and I showed her my job. After giving her a tour, we left the ship to see her life in NYC. Her office had a full view of Central Park. Eventually, I picked up on the fact that she was rich. I will never forget when she told me in her strong accent, "I came to this country with a bag and no phone to call home. I had a choice to live at the top of the Empire State Building or under the Brooklyn Bridge."

There are no words in the dictionary to express how that moment impacted my life.

The next day, as my ship left the pier, my eyes were full of tears. I couldn't believe I survived hardship and death to settle for average. I had been exposed to a better life I knew I deserved. At that moment, I decided to leave the military. I would have rather been homeless than give up on being the best version of myself.

I had about two years to put myself in the best financial position before being honorably discharged from the service. So, I paid off all my debt with the cash I had saved, including my car and college loans. I cut out my "wants," such as clothing, shoes, and dining out. As I continued to live conservatively, I eventually bought a home in a promising area to become a landlord. Then, I started a watch business. Before I knew it, I was out of the service and headed up the highway to Philadelphia.

I had never visited Philadelphia until the morning I moved into my new home. The truth is, I allowed someone to influence me that Philly would give me that bright-lights feeling. Initially, New York City was the plan until I realized it would be a culture shock for a small-town guy like me. Philadelphia was a major city but not as big. As I drove into Philadelphia, I saw the beautiful skyline, and all I could do was smile because I was officially on my pursuit of happiness.

As you can see, I didn't always have it figured out. I experienced several years of depression, confusion, and pain. I remained complacent because complacency was what I knew.

However, our comfort zones can restrict us from access, growth, and seizing opportunities. You may not always have the answers, but you will never find them when watching from the sidelines and judging the players in the game.

The time has come to unlock your true potential and activate your inner greatness. From this point forward, decide to step out of your comfort zone. Walk with me.

THE KEY TO UNLOCKING YOUR POTENTIAL

At some point, people become comfortable and settle. You may wonder how or why. Well, we're all unique, meaning my challenges are different than your challenges, and how we respond to those challenges differs too. For two years, I was challenged to write this book because it required a lot of work. You may have tried to enroll into school again but given up. Someone else is a product of their environment, and their childhood community is all they know. But what we have in common is that we want to find a way to break out of our comfort zones. I understand that it's easier to operate within your comfort zone because you're seasoned in that area. Your comfort zone is what you know life to be for you. If poverty is your comfort zone, you accept that you're poor and life isn't fair. But what about the fear of failure? Fear of failure happens when self-doubt overrules confidence. Another common comfort zone is keeping a small circle of friends. Poverty, fear of failure, and a small circle of friends are three examples of challenges you must overcome in your comfort zone.

POVERTY

Poverty is the lack of the financial resources to enjoy the minimum standards of living. Being poor is an unfortunate situation many have experienced at some point. A poverty-stricken environment is a challenge to navigate. Poverty is a vicious cycle, leading to crime and mental illness, which leads to desperation and hopelessness. Your zip code could cause you to be alienated and discriminated against because of a few knuckleheads. Have you ever heard of the saying "it only takes a few bad apples to spoil the bunch?" A study found that only 6 percent of the entire population in Chicago was responsible for 70 percent of the non-fatal gun violence in the city. What makes Chicago dangerous for the rest of the neighborhood is that a small amount of exposure to violence increases one's risk of becoming a victim (Papachristos et al. 2015). If you're a victim of violence, you're more likely to be victimized again or become involved (Everytown Research & Policy 2022).

Crime and mental illness are the risks people think of when living in poverty, but the circulation of misinformation holds back most ambitious people. The information circulating in the neighborhood runs the risk of bias and incorrectness due to a lack of education. Access is the cost of being misinformed. You should want to surround yourself with people more intelligent than you. If you repeat, reference, or share false information, you'll be viewed as unreliable and unbeneficial. Guess who else will deny you access? Banks for business loans, talent recruiters, and potential business partners. A lack of education puts you at greater risk of being misinformed. Please be mindful and skeptical of the information you digest. The following picture from the US Census Bureau shows the correlation between poverty and education (Semega et al. 2020, 57).

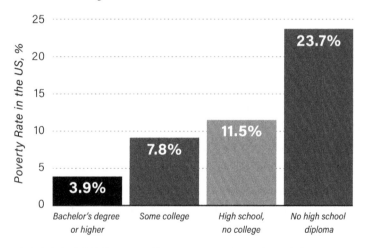

Population limited to individuals aged 25 or older. **Source:** Income and Poverty in the United States: 2019, Current Population Reports, U.S. Census Bureau. Revised September 2021.

THE FEAR OF FAILURE

The fear of failure is a constant battle everyone faces throughout their journey. Don't let the fear of failure stop you from achieving your goals. When an inventor brings their imagination to life, it's a sign that their confidence defeated their fear of failure. When entrepreneurs open for business, it means their confidence overcame their negative thoughts.

The fear of failure destroys the possibility of growth and success. No one becomes successful without failure. Did you know that Walt Disney was fired from one of his first jobs because he wasn't creative enough? Yes, Walt Disney, the founder of the greatest chain of theme parks in the world with the most magical experience every child craves (Gillett 2015). When fear of failure creeps within, remember that the worst someone can tell you is no. The answer "no" means you should create better value or find someone that values your talent. Defeat your fear of failure with confidence.

SMALL CIRCLE NETWORK

I know everyone has heard, "It's not about what you know but who you know."

Well, those words are true.

The only time I have ever received an interview from a corporate company was because of a referral. Every person that referred me was someone I met, and during that interaction, I was kind to them. My childhood friends didn't put me in that space. Your small, immediate circle of friends is your comfort zone. Sure, they may be successful and intelligent, but they may not necessarily be the answer to your needs. The answers to your questions are walking past you when you're out running errands.

Yes, a stranger could be your answer. Kindness will open just about any door you could imagine. Some conversations will go further than others, so when you find a common interest with someone, open the door for opportunity.

In 2016, a survey uncovered that 85 percent of all jobs were filled via networking (LinkedIn 2016). If you are established, help someone. When we help each other succeed, we build a stronger economy.

GET COMFORTABLE WITH BEING UNCOMFORTABLE

If you ever feel comfortable with what you're doing in life, challenge yourself to overcome an obstacle that doesn't feel second nature. I understand that stepping outside your comfort zone is difficult because it requires physical and emotional energy, but that's where change occurs. In the following chart, notice the correlation between time and change.

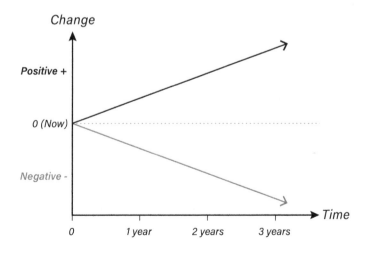

What does this chart mean? Well, if you continue to make positive changes over time by repeatedly making good decisions, you'll get closer to your goals. Let me say that again: If you continue to make positive changes over time by repeatedly making good decisions, you'll get closer to your goals.

EFFECTIVE AND EFFICIENT

The most important asset you can control is you.

The most important asset you can't control is time.

If you use time efficiently, you'll operate more effectively. However, if you're indecisive about progression, you need to face yourself in the mirror and uncover why you struggle with operating at your best. Never forget that you owe your highest energy and effort to yourself. Too many people reach their final years wishing they had done things differently.

Are you in favor of being the best version of yourself today?

If so, keep walking with me.

Time management is how you become effective and efficient at achieving your goals. You need to know what you want and how you plan to get there. Before I go to bed at night, I use a whiteboard to write down all the goals I need to complete the next day. At the end of the next day, I write my goals for the day after. The goals you complete every day will eventually lead to your end goal. My daily goals also involve going to the gym and reading some of my favorite books. So, I must prioritize based on importance and time sensitivity. The following are a few crucial factors regarding time management:

1. *Accountability:* Plan accordingly. Choose to be early.

2. *Externalize:* Never bottle your thoughts up in your head. Get them out on paper or your phone.

3. *Goals and tracking metrics:* Make sure your daily goals are small and achievable.

4. *Communication:* Ask questions if you need help. The more extensive your network, the more choices you have for resources.

5. *Motivation:* Never forget why you're doing this.

LEVERAGE YOUR ACCOMPLISHMENTS TO MOTIVATE YOURSELF

When you begin to achieve your goals, be sure to applaud yourself. Be proud of your accomplishments. You'll never get that time back. So, honor your achievements. I frame all my certificates, recognitions, news articles, diplomas, and degrees because I achieved those accomplishments in exchange for my most valuable asset: time. When I question myself or lose focus, I look at the wonderful things I've done, reaffirming I'm on the right track. Those achievements, big and small, are positive changes and steps I took to reach bigger goals.

Remember, all of us are unique and have our own stories. Don't compare yourself to someone else. My obstacles were different from anyone else's, including those who lived under the same roof as me. Measure your success based on your career path and your goals to become successful. Don't become discouraged as you become older. Older people are wise and experienced. Leo Goodwin founded GEICO insurance at the age of 50, and the face of Kentucky Fried Chicken, Colonel Sanders, was 62 when he franchised KFC (Gillet 2015).

Let's move on to the topic that brought you here: moola. Money. Benjamins. Those George Washingtons!

Jokes aside, be familiar with the reasons you want more money. There are two reasons people usually read personal finance books:

1. They want to make more money.

2. They want to make better decisions with their money.

Reason #2 is wise.

Reason #2 is the main topic of financial literacy and money management. It's not about what you can make but what you can keep. But first, let's uncover a resounding answer to an important question: Why do you want more money? Typically, when asking this question, I receive a generic response such as "To give my kids a better life" or "I want better for myself." Although those statements may be factual, you must go into more detail. For example, what do you want to change about your kids' living conditions? What needs do you want to fulfill? Being more specific about what you plan to accomplish will add more substance to your goal and allow you to visualize what needs to be completed.

A common reason some folks want more money is to have

nicer things. When receiving or earning more money, people often buy those nicer things and then want more money to do the same thing. But that doesn't change their living conditions, and those people become slaves to a lifestyle. Worse, and most importantly, they're still working for money instead of making money work for them.

The more they make, the more they spend.

Some spend more unnecessarily than others. When making more money, the brand of clothes they wear changes. People tend to shop for more expensive cars, too. We become more willing to participate in things that seemed too expensive in the past. People begin to treat themselves because they "deserve it." Folks become victims of their emotions.

All the hopeless romantics know what I'm talking about!

I'm taking no prisoners by sharing these truths, and I don't want to hear any of the excuses you come up with as to why you handle money carelessly.

A sale in your favorite department store makes you emotionally excited. Now you want to buy everything you like. A car salesman tells you they're having a Labor Day sale, and you go full throttle into making a purchase.

"No money down, and we'll give you extra money on a trade-in," he exclaims, but that doesn't change the fact that you're buying a depreciating asset that will lose over half of its value by the time you pay it off. You dive headfirst into the sale and flush tens of thousands of dollars down the toilet because a car was your favorite color and the car salesman had a "deals" sticker on his shirt. Tighten up!

Let's say you own stock (equity investments in publicly traded companies), and the stock market is drowning. The moment you turn on the news, the newscaster will make you think you're about to lose everything. You become emotional and decide to sell your stock. The next day, the stock market recovers, but you sold your stock and lost money because you were emotionally unstable.

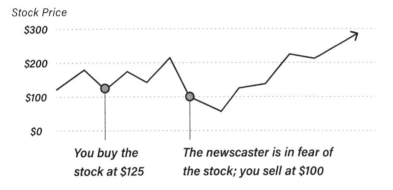

Stock Price

You buy the stock at $125

The newscaster is in fear of the stock; you sell at $100

In this example, you bought a valuable stock at $125 per share. The next day, the stock market is red (meaning it lost money). The newscaster mentions your company on TV and expresses their fears about the company. So, you decide to jump ship and sell. The next day, the stock market recovers, and the company's stock price rebounds. In this example, you lost money because you couldn't control your emotions.

What about real estate? There are deals everywhere because there will always be one of the four Ds taking place somewhere in the country:

1. Death

2. Disaster

3. Divorce

4. Debt

In those four situations, you're more than likely to find someone trying to get rid of their property and move on in life.

In these examples, I showed you how emotions could affect the results of your investments. Always make sure you control your feelings and never make impulsive decisions. Patience is a virtue. When referring to investments, bad decisions can cost you everything you've worked to earn.

STUDENT OF LIFE

This is the end of the chapter but not the end of your journey. Your mindset is the most crucial topic when making critical decisions. The best decisions aren't always free. Cheaper doesn't mean better. Keep an open mind and continue to learn how to make intelligent decisions about investments, ownership, outsourcing, and life. The day you quit learning is the day you begin dying. Now, let's walk the talk.

List three of the most important concepts in this section.

1. ....

2. ....

3. ....

No one becomes successful without ....

....

What comfort zone (being overweight, overspending, unemployment, and so forth) do you want to overcome?

....

Brainstorm three viable solutions to address the above-mentioned problem.

1. ....

2. ....

3. ....

Sometimes you must unlearn and relearn. What does this mean, and why is it important?

....

....

How do you achieve your end goals? Circle the answer that applies to your life.

a. Keep the goal in the back of your mind.

b. I don't worry about it. It will eventually come.

c. Break down the end goal into smaller, achievable goals.

d. Goals aren't that important.

PART II

BUDGET

Budgeting is the most important conversation we often don't have when discussing money. To reiterate, a budget is the most valuable yet underutilized tool with the potential to change your life. You must have a budget. A budget is a system that structures the cash flow of your money. With a budget, you know what money comes in, and you know what goes out. Based on your financial goals, you should adjust your budget periodically to ensure you're on track to accomplish your goals. Once you build the system, you can expect to produce wealth.

THE BASIC ELEMENTS OF A BUDGET

Bear with me. I'll start with the basics to ensure you're in the know across the board. These basics will qualify you to be the critical thinker and financial analyst at the dinner table. With them, you'll have the ability to troubleshoot your budget and figure out what's going on in your household. Let's get activated!

A budget is broken down into three major parts:

1. Income

2. Expenses

3. Net Income

Net income is the money left over after paying your expenses and Uncle Sam (an employer usually takes out taxes).

The following example will demonstrate the relationship between the three major parts of a budget and how to find value within your budget. Follow along as I make what seems complicated digestible.

John "Money" Doe makes $1,000 each month and pays $500 in expenses. John has $500 of net income (NI) left over. Here's a poor illustration for your amusement:

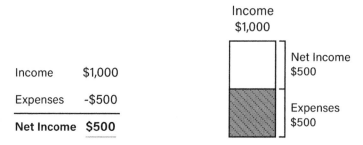

How can John "Money" Doe increase his net income? (Hint: There are two ways.)

1. ....

2. ....

There are two ways to increase your net income (NI):

1. Increase your income.
2. Decrease your expenses.

Take a minute to think about those two strategies. What do others usually choose? We like to burn money, and we want more money to burn. So, we find other ways to make more money. What does that look like?

RUNNING THE BAG UP (CONTINUED EXAMPLE)

John "Money" Doe chooses option one (increase your income). Currently, he makes a total of $2,000 each month from his job and side hustle. His total expenses remain at $500. Now, he has $1,500 left over. Notice that when John makes more dough, he doesn't spend more dough. In this case, John adds more value to his budget by increasing his income.

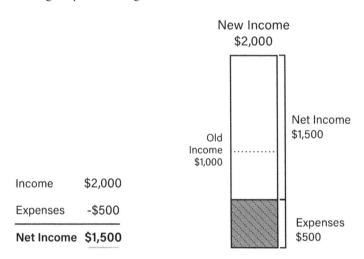

Let's talk income, or what we like to call "running up a check," for a minute. Everybody wants more money, but the truth about making more money is ugly. The truth is so ugly that people capitalize on social media to make their life appear glamorous. These influencers create courses full of bullcrap that leave people feeling confused with no results.

How would I know?

Well, I've spent well over $10,000 on courses full of worthless information. I can tell you how to make a lot more money right here, right now, but are you ready to accept the ugly truth?

The first tip about making more money is to increase your human capital. Human capital is a combination of your knowledge and skills that can be used to help others achieve their goals. This brings me to a key point: you don't have to go to college to succeed, but you must educate yourself within an industry or field. Education will help you understand the foundation of the work. The more hands-on you are with the work, the more skilled you will become.

Ask a successful barber who started out butchering their friends' heads for free.

Ask a successful chief financial officer (CFO) who started many years ago by sitting at their first desk, lost in a thousand emails and a stack of paperwork.

Ask a successful realtor how many houses they sold when they started.

The more skilled and knowledgeable you become in any given field of work, the more valuable your time becomes.

Speaking of realtors, my first property manager (before I hired him) came to my house in 2017. I wanted to get to know him before I passed the possession of my largest asset into his control. I asked him how he got into the property management business. He explained that he was a realtor and continued to have clients ask him if he knew anyone who could manage their properties with tenants. He didn't know anyone . . . until he took on the task. At that time, he managed nearly a dozen properties. In August 2020, his assistant told me that he had about 300 properties.

That's amazing, right?

This man was knowledgeable in the real estate industry and identified a niche market in his field. He created a business and became wealthy.

Notice that I mentioned a niche market and how he created a business to fill a void. Remember this: People will pay you to solve their problems. When you're knowledgeable and skilled, people will value your work. Word of mouth travels at the speed of light. Customers will recommend you to others, and business will eventually flow to you, which will increase the value of your time and work.

Most importantly, identify what you love to do. Don't sell yourself short by doing gigs to make ends meet. Don't go to a job every day, cussing people out under your breath as a part of your daily routine. That's a sign that you're not serving your purpose. Remember, your happiness is most important. If it doesn't make you happy, it doesn't deserve your time. Again, time is the most valuable asset you can't control. Some people are paid for what they love and make nearly nothing, but they feel happy. Before I almost died, I woke up and realized I hadn't found happiness in the life I had chosen. Not everyone gets the opportunity of a second chance, so don't expect one. Bring out that best version of you now.

Let's move forward to examine the second way to increase your net income, which is to reduce your expenses.

STAY DOWN TO COME UP—SHED COST (CONTINUED EXAMPLE)

John "Money" Doe makes a total of $1,000 a month from his job. John cuts some of his costs and reduces his total expenses to $250. He has $750 left over. When John saves dough by reducing expenses, his net income increases. In this case, John adds more value to his budget by decreasing his expenses.

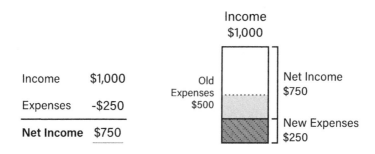

Income	$1,000
Expenses	-$250
Net Income	**$750**

Who am I to write a book and tell you to cut your spending? I don't even know you!

However, I also want you to understand the benefits of being disciplined with money. Let me start by mentioning the control you have over your life. A lot of the money you spend has an influence behind it. Our family and friends make it seem like every event is more important than the last 1,000 events we've attended with them. Our precious little monsters are hard to say no to, especially when they give us puppy eyes. Last but not least, breaking old habits is hard. Whoever needs to read this, there's nothing wrong with the shoes on your feet. If your shoes don't have holes in them, you don't need to buy another pair. Based on a few of those situations (attending events, spoiling your kiddos, and buying new shoes), how much do you think you've spent?

Probably hundreds or even thousands, right? Imagine if you were bold enough to say "no" more often. How much of a difference would you notice in your bank account? Try it out for one month. Discipline yourself to say no to unnecessary things to gain more control over your financial life.

The next time you decide to spend money on an item, determine that item's lifespan and long-term value. People commonly get tripped up with new cars, a depreciating asset that loses most of its value when you drive it off the lot and is worth nearly nothing in five to ten years. You will come across many people with really nice things that are a waste of money, and although those items are nice, I challenge you to stay focused.

You might say, "Why shouldn't I be influenced? Why can't I spend?"

First, you don't know if that influencer is financially literate. So, don't assume someone knows what they're doing with money just because they have it.

Second, you don't know if they paid cash or took out a loan, are in good financial standing, or are behind on payments.

In 2017, I had a wristwatch start-up company. I searched Instagram high and low for thriving entrepreneurs sporting foreign cars from their hard work. I planned to leverage their lifestyles as the face of my brand. I needed them to expeditiously generate content to create campaigns on social media. I didn't expect so many of them to make excuses to delay the content because they hadn't picked up the rental car yet. Yes, rental car. I was mind blown! They delivered some cool pictures, but the wait was longer than agreed upon because the car wasn't in their possession.

Well, guess what?

Some of them were verified on Instagram, which completely blew my mind.

Last, but most importantly, who cares what others think? Your goals are uniquely for you. Don't allow material items to knock you off your savings game. You have an end goal regarding your finances, so stay focused.

Before we wrap up cutting costs, I want you to know what my mom used to say to me: "Boy, you better get out of my face. You have food on the table, clothes on your back, and a roof over your head."

Essentially, she was explaining that I have all my basic needs. Anything else was extra, and she was right.

Let me ask you: how much are you willing to sacrifice today to secure your tomorrow? If you live every day like it's your last, you'll have to work when you're supposed to be retired. Commit to making better spending decisions. I believe in you. I just need you to believe in yourself.

Let's continue walking.

LEAN, GREEN MONEY MACHINE (CONTINUED EXAMPLE)

John "Money" Doe makes a total of $2,000 a month from his job and side hustle. John cut some of his costs and reduced his total expenses to $250. He has $1,750 left over. In this example, John has more money left than in all the other examples. John adds more value to his budget by increasing his income and decreasing his expenses.

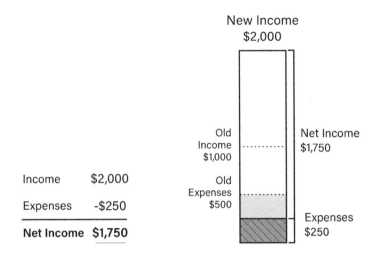

This is what it looks like when you're doing everything you can to maximize the value in your budget by increasing your income and reducing your expenses. John "Money" Doe is starting to look like Floyd "Money" Mayweather, except he's missing some zeros, but you get the point.

I'm good at making money, and I know many people who are better than me in that department, but my skills in cutting costs give me deep pockets too. Increasing your income can take time. Creating another income stream can take time. But you can cut costs today. Get rid of non-essential bills and subscriptions. Maximize the value in your budget. Remember, your financial goals are uniquely for you. Focus on you.

DETAILED BUDGET

Below is a simple equation we've used in the previous examples for John "Money" Doe. That equation breaks down into a detailed budget essential to wealth building. Look at how the total income is broken down into multiple incomes, and the total expenses are broken down into individual expenses.

Income (monthly)	
1st Job	$1,500
2nd Job	$1,000
Side Hustle	$500
Total	**$3,000**

Expenses (monthly)	
Rent/Mortgage	$750
Car	$150
Car Insurance	$100
Phone	$50
Water	$50
Electricity	$100
Food	$200
Gas	$100
Total	**$1,500**

Income	$3,000
Expenses	-$1,500
Net Income	**$1,500**

BUDGET TIPS TO REMEMBER

1. Don't avoid cutting unnecessary expenses.

2. If an expense drains your money, it's time to downgrade or get rid of it.

3. There's nothing wrong with using pencil and paper to write out your budget.

4. After you pay your bills from your checking account, allow a few days to pass for the remaining funds to be withdrawn.

INCOME TIPS

1. Don't overestimate your monthly income—meaning, don't use the highest expected amount from your paycheck. If your paychecks vary, use the lowest amount you expect to receive. You would rather have more money on payday than less money than you expected. Be modest.

2. Don't add unlikely income streams to your budget (don't fall into false hope); for example, money others owe you. Although the borrower might pay you back, don't include this money in your budget. Another example is money you "plan" to make, as in you plan to deliver pizza in the near future, but you haven't earned money yet. In both examples, the risk of uncertainty could negatively offset your budget because you were expecting money you didn't receive or make.

EXPENSE TIPS

Have you ever been broke during one part of the month because your paycheck was swallowed by most of your bills, but when you received your next paycheck, you had a pocket full of money? Stabilize your paychecks by factoring in your total monthly expenses in each paycheck. How often you get paid is important. Divide your total monthly expenses by the number of times you get paid in a month. In the budget above, for example, the total monthly expenses equaled $1,500.

Weekly	*Bi-Weekly*	*Monthly*
$1,500 ÷	$1,500 ÷	$1,500 ÷
4 paychecks	2 paychecks	1 paychecks
$375	**$750**	**$1,500**

Those are the amounts of money you need to set aside from each paycheck to afford your monthly expenses.

Add each debt payment (credit card, personal, school loans, etc.) as an expense line item into your budget. Don't combine them into one expense.

Do not underestimate expenses. It's okay to overestimate each expense by a few dollars. There's nothing wrong with a margin of error.

Try to pay all your bills on the first or fifteenth. Don't make your budget a full-time job by paying unexpected bills every few days.

THE MONEY LEFT OVER IS THE GAME CHANGER

The budget is the most important reason for why I wrote this book. Maximizing the value in your budget will open the door of opportunity to change your life by allowing you to make good decisions with the money you have leftover.

So, what do you do with the money left over from the budget?

You allocate it.

You thought I was playing earlier when I said you'll be the financial analyst at the dinner table? Well, I'm excited about the impact that's about to take place in your life.

THE ALLOCATION OF MONEY

The ability to properly allocate money is a valuable skill. This means you assign money to different groups. Do you remember the saying "never put all of your eggs in one basket?" Allocation is when you put your eggs in different baskets. We allocate money by percentage (%). Allocation is simpler than it sounds. Check out this example:

Let's say I had $1,500 of NI or money left over from my budget. Based on my goals, I want to:

- Spend 10% on having fun with my friends.

- Set aside 10% to give my kids a good Christmas.

- Invest 30% in my stock portfolio.

- Stash 50% for the down payment on a house.

Spending		Christmas		Invest		Save for House		Total
10%	+	10%	+	30%	+	50%	=	100%
$150		$150		$450		$750		$1,500

Remember, when you allocate your money, don't leave your NI in the same account you use to pay your bills. Separate the money by transferring funds to different banks or brokerages or using the good old envelope method. The envelope method uses multiple envelopes representing the different groups of money to store cash. The bottom line is that you don't want to confuse the different groups of money. This isn't rocket science, right?

It's okay if it takes you two or three tries to read and analyze this chapter. It took me nearly a decade to organize this amount of information. So, please, don't feel discouraged. As you can see, it's deeper than living below your means. Living below your means is generic advice people yell out to avoid money management conversations. The conversation about money management is about how you effectively align your finances to meet your goals. That's the only way to determine your level of financial success. There are short-term and long-term goals, so don't expect this to be an overnight process.

Let's keep stepping.

PART III

RISK
MANAGEMENT

DO YOU KNOW THE QUICKEST WAY TO LOSE IT ALL?

In 1997, Notorious B.I.G released the hit single "Mo Money, Mo Problems." In the chorus, he wants to know what else do people want him because it's evident more problems arise the more money he accumulates. I agree with Biggie. You have more to lose when you turn your budget into a cash cow, level up, and accumulate assets. In other words, as you increase your reward, you inherently increase your risk of loss. Why earn a lot just to lose it all?

I don't plan on losing anything, and you shouldn't either.

This is why we practice risk management: to reduce or prevent the possibility of loss. You can't accurately predict when you'll take a loss. No one says, "I'm happy my car is going to break down next week and my house is going to be set ablaze with all of my belongings inside." Don't be naïve and think tragedy can't happen to you. Risk management is fundamental in the process of building wealth. Limit your risk exposure. Remember, it's not about what you can make; it's about what you can keep. Let me show you.

NO IFS, ANDS, OR BUTS

Unfortunately, most people can't afford to pay for everything in cash. This includes buying new organs and limbs, paying for hospital stays, replacing a home, and buying a car. If you can't replace it with cash, you must insure it. If you're just beginning your financial literacy journey, please know the four types of insurance every person should have:

1. Medical insurance

2. Life insurance

3. Car insurance

4. Homeowners insurance

MEDICAL INSURANCE

You're a walking liability. At any moment, you could become ill, break a bone, or have a bodily emergency. Let me quantify this for you: according to Healthcare.gov, a broken leg can cost up to $7,500, the average three-night stay in the hospital is $30,000, and comprehensive cancer treatments can cost hundreds of thousands of dollars (2019). Do you think any of those amounts are cheaper than paying a few hundred dollars a month for medical insurance?

LIFE INSURANCE

Conversations about death seem forbidden. Do you want to ruin the vibe? Bring up life insurance when a parent asks what their child will do with all that birthday money. Besides my ignorant jokes, life insurance is something you want to talk about with a professional. My needs are different from yours, so the amount of life insurance you might want will differ from mine. Still, everyone must have enough coverage for funeral arrangements, to pay off all debts to avoid any debtor claims on your estate, and to replace your income if you have any dependents. You don't need anything complex with bells and whistles. Life insurance isn't an investment vehicle. Purchase it for its sole purpose. Shop around and find professionals to help you.

CAR INSURANCE

There's no such thing as having a car without car insurance. An uninsured vehicle is unacceptable under any circumstances. Being uninsured while driving leaves you too exposed to financial risk. Imagine saving thousands of dollars at the height of your life only to lose it all in a lawsuit because of a car accident. If you have outstanding car payments, full-coverage car insurance is mandatory. If your car is paid off, my rule of thumb is to have full coverage insurance if you can't afford to buy another vehicle in cash without causing turbulence in your life. If your car is cheap and a beater, you're fine with liability insurance.

Why?

I would imagine no one wants to have high monthly car insurance payments for a beater car. Eventually, the accumulated monthly cost of the insurance would surpass the vehicle's value. If you have a low monthly payment, you have a high deductible of $500 or $1,000. In an accident, the price to fix your car may be higher than the value of your vehicle. But, please understand, if you choose liability insurance, make sure you're financially ready and able to replace the car at all times.

HOMEOWNERS INSURANCE

Houses are the largest assets owned by the middle class. Severe storms and disasters are inevitable. Make sure you're covered by insurance if you own a home. If you rent, check into renter's insurance that fits your needs.

I once had a challenging time with a property I own. The tenant periodically noticed a small puddle on the floor. Eventually, after sending multiple plumbers and not receiving a clear explanation, I realized they weren't equipped for that type of work. So, I paid for a company that specialized in leak detection. I found out the leak was coming from a different room and caused nearly $30,000 of damage. Luckily, my insurance covered most of the tab.

The following year, the same tenant had a career change and left the area. Once my property managers viewed the vacant property, a lot of work needed to happen before another tenant arrived—about $10,000 worth of work to keep my rent at a premium price on the market. It was unpleasant to bleed so much cash at that time, but guess what? I was prepared. I was properly insured, and there was plenty of cash in the stash for those types of moments.

CASH IN THE STASH

We all know what a rainy day fund is, right? A rainy day fund is money you set aside for emergencies. You need to build that fund as fast and efficiently as possible, meaning you should rapidly build your stash, but make sure to take care of the home front as well. Don't starve your family to add more to the stash.

But you should expect to make sacrifices within your budget. Set your rainy day savings on autopilot by treating it as a monthly expense in your budget.

Stash away a minimum of 10 to 20 percent of your paycheck. You must understand that the amount of money you keep in your emergency fund will differ from others. Again, we're all unique. A married family with children won't have the same emergency fund as a high school graduate. A good rule of thumb for a minimum amount in your emergency fund is $1,000 for each adult and $500 for each child. As your net worth grows, make sure this stash grows too. Another rule of thumb is that your emergency fund should cover three to six months of your total expenses. Either stash the cash or wire the money to another bank you don't usually use.

According to the rule-of-thumb minimum, how much do you need to stash away for your rainy day fund?

Ultimately, how much money should be in your rainy day fund?

How much of your paycheck (at a minimum) should you stash away each month?

%

SECURE THE BAG

You're now equipped to minimize your exposure to risk. You're capable of being your safety net when things go wrong in life. You don't have to make embarrassing calls to ask others for help anymore. Instead, you have the knowledge to be dependable enough for others to call upon. Managing risk isn't a moneymaker; it's a money saver. Don't lose everything you've worked for because you avoided financial responsibility. Again, it's not about what you can make; It's about what you can keep. Secure the bag.

PART IV

DEBT MANAGEMENT

CREDIT – CASH = DEBT

Am I the only person who argues with the radio in the morning? As I'm driving, I hear a car dealership ad: "Bad credit or no credit, all you need is a pay stub of $200 a week, and you'll leave the lot today in your new ride!"

Are they crazy?

In 2022, the average car loan in the US for a used vehicle was $526 a month (Betterton 2023).

Let's say you found good, full-coverage car insurance for $170. If you make $1,600-ish a month ($400/week), why would you add a $696 fixed cost to your budget for the next five years? That would eat up over 40 percent of your money. So, my first question to anyone that asks me to help improve their credit is "why?" Credit is a tool used to access debt. In reality, credit is a tool we use to abuse debt.

According to an article from Experian, consumer debt has reached a record high of over $16 trillion. Included in this consumer debt dollar amount is auto-loan debt, which reached a record-high of $1.4 trillion (Horymski 2023). This means more people are increasingly looking for ways to borrow money to purchase things they cannot afford.

Debt is a subject people hate to talk about, but it must be confronted before becoming a slave to creditors. I understand that we all make mistakes and can admit that our financial decisions are mindless at times, but our duty as responsible adults is to right our wrongs. You may have irresponsibly used credit in the past, but ultimately, you're damaging your financial reputation. You don't want to go the rest of your life looking over your shoulder, hoping no one garnishes your checks or repossesses your car. If you're in debt, take control of your life.

I'll say it again: Take control of your life.

Check your feelings, desires, and carelessness at the door because two steps forward can quickly turn into ten steps back. We're talking about the deterioration of wealth due to the irresponsible usage of debt, excessive spending on depreciating assets and worthless items, and long-term interest costs from debt. Therefore, debt management is more important to address than investments. I'm going to show you how to view debt and get rid of it, answer valid questions regarding the use of debt, and build your credit score.

HOW TO VIEW DEBT

There are two types of debt in this world (Tony Montana voice):

1. Good debt
2. Bad debt

So, how do you tell the difference?

Good debt delivers a return on your investment or solves a greater issue in the most efficient way.

Bad debt is simply a bad decision, even if it had the potential to be good debt.

The fine line between good and bad debt is the ability to think critically and exercise self-discipline. You should have multiple questions regarding how to spend your hard-earned money on any big purchase you make. Even though it may be shiny, and you feel pressured to decide, self-restraint and the maturity to walk away will save you money and build wealth.

Check out a few examples of good debt and the features that draw the fine line to separate them from bad debt:

Good debt delivers a return on your investment in the most efficient way: This involves an asset with a long-term value or that helps generate income. In other words, this is an investment.

For example, a car can be considered good debt. It delivers a return by getting you to and from work, where you generate income. However, you don't need a new luxury car to get you to work, and buying an SUV as a single person with no family is inefficient. You'll pay more for unutilized space, gas, and maintenance. At that point, it's bad debt. But, if you have an SUV for your family or a pickup truck for work, it's good debt because it maximizes the efficiency of your vehicle. Remember, if you can afford it, buy it used with cash because there's a cost to borrow.

A home is considered good debt. In most cases, it's better to own than rent. If you decide to buy a house and can afford it, go for it! Just be mindful of the costs associated with it, like the down payment, maintenance, repairs, and the cost of selling.

Speaking of the cost to sell—in 2018, the average house in the US sat on the market between sixty-five and ninety-three days from listing to closing (Zillow 2019). That's roughly three months before the seller could cut ties with the costs associated with that home. I emphasize the responsibility of being a homeowner, but knowing you're an owner is even more rewarding. Just like an oversized car is inefficient and crosses the line to be considered bad debt, there's such a thing as too much house. Usually, you realize you have too much house when you can't afford the monthly mortgage or haven't seen certain parts of the home in weeks.

I've owned and rented property for the last six years with a solid 20 percent return on my investment. Don't let someone tell you homeownership is a bad idea. Be sure your budget is bulletproof and your rainy day fund is locked and loaded.

Good debt *solves a greater cause*: Not all your good decisions with debt usage will bring money or equity. Sometimes, it's about taking care of the family. I won't call decisions like this bad debt because I don't encourage putting a dollar amount on life. I understand that insurance doesn't always cover everything. Don't second-guess taking care of the family. A heart, lung, limb, and life are priceless. If your insurance and cash can't cover the costs, don't second-guess using debt to save your family. Just be smart and explore your options before signing a high-interest loan.

LARGE DEBTS ARE PAID OVER TIME, NOT OVERNIGHT
Paying back long-term debt isn't something you should expect to achieve overnight. This is a process to chip away at with consistency. For many, debt is a roadblock to financial freedom, from low-income households to deep-pocketed millionaires.

There are a few strategies I would suggest using to pay off debt, and there's one strategy I'll never use. Without further ado, let me show you how to attack debt.

Note: *These strategies require a solid budget.*

The following rule applies to the strategies below: Never pay the minimum payment on a loan unless it's a part of a strategy. That's next to sinful, equivalent to someone robbing a bank and one of the victims yelling as they're leaving, "Hey! You forgot my wallet, Sir!"

Don't be an idiot. Keep your money. Creditors will prolong a loan to collect as much interest as possible. You're being robbed if you pay the minimum every month. However, in the recommended strategy, you'll discover that paying the minimum on some loans is okay because it works toward a greater cause. Let's take a look.

Strategy #1: *Debt Avalanche*: Strategies #1 and #2 have been around for decades, before my mother even thought about giving my dad a shot to see what he got, but I digress. The debt avalanche is a proven debt strategy that tells you to aggressively pay off your loan with the highest interest rate first while making the minimum payment on your other loans (aggressive meaning that you take all your extra money from your budget and attack that sucka with full force). Remember, creditors make their money from the interest you pay for borrowing money. The higher the interest rate, the more creditors will make off you on the loan. This strategy is solid, but I'll later share why it's not preferrable in most cases.

Strategy #2: Debt Snowball: I love the idea of the debt snowball. This strategy is the most popular when eliminating debt. With this strategy, you take all your extra money and attack the smallest loan amount first while paying the minimum on the others. Once you pay off the smallest loan, you move to the next smallest bill. You take all your extra money you started with plus the minimum payment from the last bill to pay the next bill. You continue this process as you pay off all your debt. I understand that it sounds complicated, so I fashioned the example below to give you some clarity. Focus on the process. Trust me. You're going to have an ah-ha moment!

In this example, let's say you have $450 a month left over from your budget after paying all your bills, including the minimum payments on your loans. You're going to apply that extra $450 to your lowest loan amount of the three debt amounts below. In this case, the lowest loan amount is your credit card, which is $500. (Note: get familiar with the chart setup before the numbers.) Let's take a look.

Types of Debts	Loan Amount	Minimum Payment	Extra Money	Total Payment	
Car Loan	$10,000	$300	0	$300	*Min. Payment*
Personal Loan	$5,000	$200	0	$200	*Min. Payment*
Credit Card	**$500**	**$50**	**$450**	**$500**	*Added the extra $450 to the min. payment of $50*

You just picked up a little momentum by paying off the lowest loan amount. Next month, take the same amount you used to pay off the credit card and use it to attack the second-lowest loan amount. Notice that the extra money used to pay off the personal loan combines the $450 previously left over with the minimum payment of $50 from the credit card you paid off.

Types of Debts	Loan Amount	Minimum Payment	Extra Money	Total Payment
Car Loan	$9,700	$300	0	$300
Personal Loan	$4,800	$200	$450+50	$700
PAID Credit Card	$0	$0	$0	$0

Okay, so you just time-traveled and paid off the personal loan. You've paid off two loans and have one left. But now you're going to use that extra $450, the $50 minimum payment from the credit card you paid off, and the $200 minimum payment from the personal loan you paid off to help pay off your car loan.

Types of Debts	Loan Amount	Minimum Payment	Extra Money	Total Payment
Car Loan	$7,900	$300	$450+$50+$200	$1,000
PAID Personal Loan	$0	$0	$0	$0
PAID Credit Card	$0	$0	$0	$0

Let's fast forward to the future, when you've finally paid the car loan off. Oh, hey there! Congratulations on paying off your imaginary debt! You're awesome, and you have a bright future ahead of you. (Yes, I talk to myself at home. In my defense, you have to speak positivity in life.)

Types of Debts	Loan Amount	Minimum Payment	Extra Money	Total Payment
PAID Car Loan	$0	$0	$0	$0
PAID Personal Loan	$0	$0	$0	$0
PAID Credit Card	$0	$0	$0	$0

I don't expect you to understand this concept the first time you look at it. I needed to look at it multiple times. Now that you've read it, go back over it, but focus on the process. Study what's going on in each column from left to right. Once you understand each column, look at each row. Be patient with yourself and analyze what's happening.

The debt snowball strategy is the most promoted debt strategy. It motivates you as you build momentum paying off debt. You pay off your smallest loans and realize progress. In the debt avalanche strategy, you start with the highest interest rate. That loan could take years to pay off if the loan amount is high. Eventually, you might lose focus and motivation. I like to ride the momentum from my small wins, which eventually achieves the larger goal. With the debt snowball strategy, you can build momentum by paying off your small loans, leading to the larger goal of being debt-free. This strategy is promoted by some of the best budget gurus in the business, whom I highly respect. This strategy works. You know what they say: if it's not broke, don't fix it.

THE UNWRITTEN DEBT LAW: ON MY TERMS

I decide my terms before I make a purchase. I determine when I'll pay off my purchases with my credit card. To use this method, you must understand your budget like an expert. When you make your own terms, you don't care when the first minimum payment is due because you've already agreed with the terms of your budget before the purchase. Check out this example:

1. I need this $300 suit for a meeting next week.

2. Before buying the suit, I think about my budget and the most efficient way to finance my suit.

3. After looking at my budget, I am confident I can afford to pay $100 immediately after the purchase and $100 from each of my next two bi-weekly paychecks. As a result, my purchase will be paid within the next month.

No matter how much you may need something, this strategy isn't worth using if you can't afford your terms. This strategy promotes financial balance. If you can't afford it, it's a bad investment. Don't force a bad investment. It's that simple.

DECISIONS MAKE THE DIFFERENCE

The decisions you make deserve more thought. Just because a sign read "SALE" doesn't change the fact that you spent money. My grandmother would come back from shopping with "clothes that will fit somebody." They weren't for a specific person. She would say, "Penney's was having a sale." In her case, she had a bad habit of shopping, like any other nurturing grandmother. Shopping is therapeutic but burns a hole in our pockets. So, when we create the habit, it's hard to shake.

Another factor that drives bad spending decisions is pride. Don't act as if you've never seen anyone play "big bank take little bank." Mirror, mirror, on the wall, who's the biggest spender of them all? My high school football coach would say, "Never get into a pissing contest with a skunk." In my interpretation, it's a skunk's nature to be wild. Don't allow your pride to put you in a position to dual with someone senseless for bragging rights. Think about that for a minute.

The last factor that drives bad spending decisions is influence. We've all bought something that we thought was cool because everybody else had it. You know, like retro Jordans. The only person that ever played like Mike because of a pair of Jordans was Calvin Cambridge in the *Like Mike* movies. If you want to be real, he didn't even pay for the beat-up shoes. The shoes also had superpowers after being electrocuted by power lines on a rainy night. Good luck with that!

I digress.

My point is that no makeup advertised will make you a Kardashian, no amount of jewelry will make your music sound better, and you won't be richer no matter how much you spend on those expensive shoes. Don't believe the hype. When you wipe off the makeup, take off all the flashy jewelry, and remove those expensive shoes, look in the mirror and tell me what you see.

Let's move on.

OVERSPENDING

If you're spending all your extra money, bring it to a halt. The more hard-earned money that's spent, the more vulnerable you become to financial instability. Even though you have extra money to spend, how prepared are you for a $1,000 emergency with your car or house? What about if your ceiling has a water leak with damages of around $7,500 tomorrow? Can you cover those types of expenses that occur over two days? We've all experienced moments when the days seem to get worse.

CONCLUSION: HOW DO I INCREASE MY CREDIT SCORE?

Let me give a little disclosure before I tell you the secret. I've never focused on credit cards or borrowing money, and I've been a part of the 800-credit-score club since I was 24 years old. Remember, a credit score shows your level of financial responsibility. "How do I increase my credit score?" has a simple answer.

Are you ready?

Fine, but don't become upset with me because it's a straightforward answer.

Reduce your debt consistently until it reaches zero and stop opening credit accounts. Paying off debt will give you a solid payment history, and your credit utilization will decrease. Pay the people you owe. I can't paint the picture any better. The truth hasn't been any prettier.

People caught in the rat race will tell you otherwise, but the truth is that debt should never be your first option, because if you're looking for more money to borrow, you don't save or make enough money. Address your budget thoroughly before relying on credit to finance your life. Remember, debt is a benefit today for a future sacrifice. That sacrifice is your ability to retire. Around retirement time, the only thing that will be working in my household is my money. If you feel me, let's walk.

Regardless of what debt payoff strategy you choose, what should you never do unless it's a part of the strategy?

Which strategy helps build momentum by removing small debt balances before large balances?

What three things contribute to making bad decisions?

1.

2.

3.

Explain the unwritten debt law.

How should you increase your credit score?

a. Consistently and rapidly pay off debt and halt opening new accounts while building a solid payment history.

b. Have someone repair your credit and wipe away your financial responsibility.

c. Make the monthly minimum payments.

d. Acquire more debt by making small purchases.

PART V

INVESTMENTS

PICTURE ME ROLLIN'

In the back of my head, I can hear Tupac's song, "Picture me rollin.'"
The instrumental is just a vibe.

Picture me rollin' in my 500 Benz down Sunset Boulevard
with the palm trees grooving to the wind. As I ride through the
neighborhood in slow motion, the homies chuck up the deuces,
paying their respect. The sunny weather makes the paint job
reflective like a bathroom mirror. Yeah . . . Picture me rollin'.

Well, at least you know I have one heck of an imagination.
I'm not even from Cali, but it's a vibe, right? However, there's a
business perspective that I want you to view the 500 Benz that
Tupac mentioned.

Hypothetically, we'll view this car as an investment vehicle
on the stock market that I'm looking to buy. So, how should I
evaluate this investment vehicle?

First, I notice the beauty of the car, the same way I see a stock
in my day-to-day activity. Whether a friend is talking about the
stock or it's all over the news, I go out of my way to look at it,
the same way we find a way to get a closer look at a car. As I
evaluate the car, I see what type of engine is under the hood. This
is equivalent to checking out a company's financial statements,
which include four basic statements:

1. A balance sheet

2. An income statement

3. A statement of retained earnings

4. A statement of cash flows

When I check out the engine's performance, I may not always understand the different terminologies, like the shaft power and calibration of the engine. To simplify all the engine specs, I want to know how much horsepower the engine has and how fast the car goes from zero to sixty. Those features are a combination of how the engine performs. I usually compare those features to competitors with similar vehicles. In the stock market, we call those features key performance indicators (KPIs). Financial statements are tough to read, just like a car engine's specs. So, many investors read KPIs and compare them to their competitor's. Some common key performance indicators include the return on assets (ROA), price-to-earnings (P/E) ratio, earnings per share (EPS), and return on equity (ROE). Those ratios should only be compared to similar companies. Be sure you're comparing apples to apples. You can't compare a luxury sports car to a heavy-duty pick-up truck. They're used for different purposes.

As I close the hood and walk around the car, I look at the wheels to ensure there are no flat tires. Tires are like media outlets. If a company has terrible media coverage, the company stock price could decline. Until the company fixes the situation, the stock will suffer. So, check the car for flat tires. Remember, just because a vehicle has a flat tire doesn't mean it's a bad car. The faster you fix the flat, the quicker you can get back on the road.

As I continue to look at the car, I realize it looks clean, but anything someone doesn't want you to see would be stuffed in the trunk. The only way to find junk is to look for it. Consider the trunk your legal issues. Many companies won't keep any of that stuff in plain view. They bury it in financial statements. Stock prices don't respond to every instance of bad news or lawsuits.

In 2012, according to Business Insider, Disney lost a $319-million lawsuit over the show *Who Wants to Be a Millionaire*. Disney was accused of hiding profits from an affiliate of the creator and licensor of the show. The only way you'll find this type of junk is to look for it. Old gym clothes are easy to clean compared to black mold. Believe it or not, the lawsuit for Disney is comparable to gym clothes in the trunk. The lawsuit was in the trunk for years and finally needed to be cleaned.

How about the lawsuit against Nike by an imprisoned pimp? In 2014, according to an article from Yahoo Sports, an imprisoned pimp serving a one hundred—year sentence sued Nike for $100 million (Woods 2020). Apparently, he felt Nike should warn their consumers that Air Jordans could be used as a dangerous weapon, which played a part in him stomping a customer's face for trying to flee without paying. In the same way you would be surprised to find items in someone's trunk, you would be surprised to find a company's hidden dirty laundry.

Now that you've evaluated the car, it's time to take a test drive. During the test drive, you'll want to make sure the car is worth buying and can drive in various weather conditions. The weather is equivalent to market conditions. Does the stock perform well in this market? Do you predict the stock will perform well in future market conditions based on past key performance indicators, current news, and future predictions?

Once you evaluate the car, you must decide if the vehicle is overvalued, undervalued, or reasonably priced. Overvalued stocks are companies that may or may not be valuable but for which the stock price is driven by sentiment. Undervalued stocks are companies with a value that's not recognized by the market. Undervalued is ideal when searching for a bang for your buck. So, be sure to shop around for similar cars that may be a better bargain.

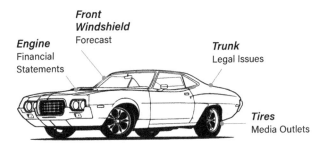

The weather is economics—can't control it.

A similar car made by a competitor.

Evaluating a stock is hard work and requires a lot of financial knowledge and analysis. Any dweeb in a suit and tie will tell you that individual stocks are risky to buy.

Why?

I'll give you a few reasons beyond the professional mumbo jumbo.

Financial knowledge: Have you opened a company's financial statements on the SEC website? Are you familiar with the different accounting methods that companies use instead of competitors' accounting methods to compare which is a better investment? Trust me, it's tricky. It's no secret that many financial analysts spend eighty to one hundred hours a week researching and evaluating different investments. Imagine working thirteen to seventeen hours a day, six days a week. The money is good, but those guys barely have time to spend it. They spend day and night at a computer making inaccurate decisions because news is constantly released that changes the impact of their investment predictions.

Diversification: The most notable way to reduce your exposure to risk is diversification. Imagine living in a state that experiences four seasons, but you only own shorts and sandals. You may feel comfortable when the sun is out in the spring and summer, but what about when it rains? You have a higher risk of being soaked from rain every time you leave your home. In the fall and winter, you run the risk of freezing your butt off with snot glaciers hanging from your nose. Also, you have a higher risk of dying from sickness and disease. Now, imagine if you were properly dressed in each season. The weather is more enjoyable. Your risk of being completely soaked in the rain is reduced when you have a raincoat, boots, and an umbrella. The snow isn't so bad with a warm coat, thick socks, and gloves. Your risk of becoming cold or sick is significantly reduced. So, can we agree it's a bad idea to have a wardrobe with only shorts and sandals compared to a diversified mix of clothes? The same goes for investments. Imagine the basic economic business cycle as the four seasons— expansion, peak, recession, and trough.

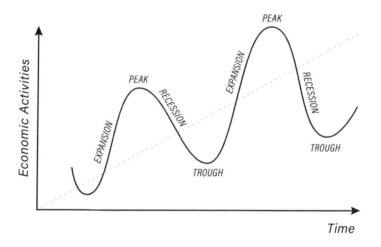

The expansion phase is when the economy is optimistic, the stock market is bullish (investors optimistic about rising share prices), and everyone is making money. (For the econ nerds, don't get literal on definitions. Just follow the example.) The peak of the expansion phase is generally at the height of a booming economy. The recession phase is when the economy takes a downturn, and the trough is when we begin recovering again.

Imagine owning stock in a luxury brand company called Furberry. This company may do well in the expansion phase because people are employed and spending money, and life is good. But, when the economy takes a turn for the worse during a recession, the market goes in the red. People are laid off from work, and there's an underlying fear across the economy. How exposed are you to a recession when your only stocks are in a luxury company?

Very exposed.

Now, imagine owning stock in Furberry and The Dollar Store. In a booming economy, more money is spent at Furberry and less at The Dollar Store. In a recession, more money will be spent at The Dollar Store instead of Furberry. In this case, you reduce your exposure to risk with diversification.

That was a small example of diversification, but your investment portfolio should have multiple investments across different sectors and industries to reduce your risk of loss. There's a way to diversify that I'll explain later in this chapter.

Oh, and don't be the person saying, "I have to diversify my wardrobe to reduce my risk of being unprepared or sick."

Cut the crap!

I know fashion junkies will use that example to fuel their bad shopping habits.

Leverage time: Evaluating investments is a full-time job, as mentioned above. If you don't genuinely love finance, don't make it your job to participate in the markets every day just for the money. I need you to be mature and hear me out because it may not make sense today, but it will later. Active participation in the markets just for the money means you have an income problem. In other words, you don't make money you desire to make. You haven't found a way to monetize your purpose and skillset. That's a problem that needs to be addressed. In the history of mankind, any time someone is in it for the money, it never ends well. Sound practices are overlooked; patience is not a virtue; and most importantly, time (our most valuable asset) is lost. Investments should be paid like a bill. The more money you make, the more you can contribute to a long-term investment. That investment will eventually grow into a large nest egg of cash and create a solid second stream of income with dividends (a term we'll discuss further).

Don't get caught in the hype: Investing isn't fun when you know what you're doing. It's a long-term game for a better life tomorrow. The amateurs creating all the hype are new to this, not true to it. Any time you ask someone truly knowledgeable in the markets where to invest your money, they're always unsure and curve the question toward very generic advice. The reason is, the more you know, the more you learn you don't know. The markets are challenging to interpret and explain. Some of the most successful people I know don't invest in individual stocks or companies. It's not because they know other places to double or triple their money. It's mainly because they want to maximize their return while reducing their level of risk exposure. Understand that the intelligent investor will know that risk looks different to everyone because our lives are unique. Some of us have kids, families, expensive health conditions, obligations, and the list goes on. So, how could someone tell you what a good stock investment would be without understanding your risk toler-ance? A middle-aged mother with three children will likely have an investment portfolio that doesn't reflect a 20-year-old college student. I'm sure mama bear would want some level of certain-ty to provide for her children and potentially send them off to college someday. The college student is more than likely looking for the next Amazon or Facebook growth stock that makes them instantly rich. Of course, screening for a home run investment comes with the risk of catastrophic loss.

Follow your purpose: If everything I said went in one ear and out the other, you need to call on a higher power. I had to nearly lose my life to realize I must stop chasing money and start following my purpose. The tricky part is finding a way to monetize what you love to do. If your passion is making money, you haven't tru-ly found your passion. You weren't born into this world to make money. Anyone determined enough can make money, but how do you want to be remembered in your absence? The foundation of building a legacy starts with your impact on others.

WHY STOCKS IN A WORLD WITH A VARIETY OF INVESTMENTS? (BENCHMARKING THE INDEXES)

The world often shares the sentiment that stocks are the best investment choice for retail investors, but have you ever won-dered why people choose stocks over other types of investments, like gold or art? We can start with real estate because the answer is a giveaway. When I reference real estate, I'm talking about long-term investments like a rental property. A rental property benefits me with tax perks, generates passive income and appreciation, and stores equity. What I'm not referring to with the term real estate are fixes and flips. Those types of gigs are income-generating activities for cash today, not an investment for tomorrow, which is comparable to trading stocks. However, people generally struggle with the cost of entering the real estate market. Traditionally, you can expect to pay closing costs and a down payment to receive the keys for a home, and those expenses include a comma. Not to mention that there are a million ways to be disqualified for a loan, including too much debt, a low credit score, a large down payment, redlining, and so forth. Beyond real estate, physical assets require more elbow grease, time, and effort to sell.

PHYSICAL ASSETS
(MAINTENANCE/STORAGE/INSURANCE AND SAFETY)

Growing up in the inner city, gold was our choice of investment. Gold looks amazing on just about everyone's skin, including mine. I bought more gold every chance I had. I wore maybe six gold necklaces at once with rings on every finger. Gold had a deeper meaning than an investment to us living in the hood. It was our shield from the world and the perfect tool of deception that we were "okay," that we'd found a level of comfort in our environment and were among the highest rank or social status within our community. Entertainment has found an interest in this way of living, and we see it in the hit music videos, popular films, and the world adopting the culture. Rap artist Mozzy always said it best, that our struggle was such a beautiful struggle. I held on to most of my gold over the years and realized I had tens of thousands of valuable pieces of jewelry. As a financially literate individual, how do I protect my interest in these physical assets?

The Value of a Physical Asset

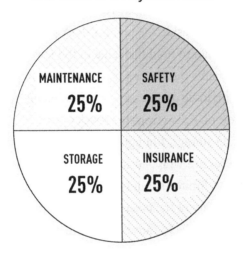

| MAINTENANCE 25% | SAFETY 25% |
| STORAGE 25% | INSURANCE 25% |

When you have physical assets, you must be mindful of their condition because they hold value. Physical assets require proper maintenance and storage. Also, the insurance and safety of the physical asset are crucial. The slightest wear and tear of any asset bites a chunk out of the value. If it goes missing, you no longer have an asset to make a profit and lose your initial investment. So, there are inherent costs to holding valuable collectibles. When you finally sell the asset, you receive a net profit. Concerning the ownership of physical assets, the takeaway is that you have to pay the cost to be the boss and hold the value while the asset increases in value.

I'll use the jewelry I've accumulated over the years as an example. I've had most of my jewelry for at least ten years. Fine jewelry isn't to my investment taste because of the seller markups on the price. Most of the cost of jewelry covers the craftsmanship of the jewelry, and we only receive a fraction of the value in weight. But that's beside the point. I don't plan to buy any more jewelry, but I plan to hold the value in the jewelry I own. I start with making sure the jewelry isn't damaged or broken. Some pieces have periodic maintenance performed on them as part of a lifetime coverage plan from the jeweler.

Regarding storage, I bought a fire-retardant safe for the jewelry. The pieces are wrapped in a soft cloth and stored inside a cool room with limited sunlight to prevent tarnishing and discoloration. The safety of the assets based on storage and the access I allow others to have to those assets is in my best interest. I pay a small monthly cost for insurance to ensure the replacement of the value of the jewelry if these assets were stolen or destroyed for any reason. Those expenses are necessary costs for me to hold the value of my assets.

My tastes are a bit better with real estate as opposed to jewelry. The same rules apply when protecting the value of the asset. As a property owner, I must maintain the exterior of the property, which includes but is not limited to cleaning the gutters, replacing the roof, cutting the grass, and power washing the siding. The interior of the property has a strong correlation with the value. Updating features and adding functionalities like central air, working lights, and a faucet that doesn't leak are the basics of interior maintenance. The safety of my rental property is my written contract signed by the tenants, which is no different than the twenty-page agreement you signed for your first apartment. You agree to pay the landlord while following a set of guidelines.

Other safety measures are burglar alarms, cameras, and smoke detectors. I don't think I need to elaborate on why those are safety measures.

The last measure that applies is insurance. Of course, I have investment property insurance to protect my largest asset. When protecting your assets, you should first identify the related expenses. Remember, there's a cost to being the boss. The biggest bosses are the ones that do it effectively and efficiently.

LIQUIDITY—HIGH-LIQUID MARKETPLACE

When you decide to sell your Xbox or gold, we call it "hood bankruptcy." Game consoles are generally sold for between $200 and $600 in store. You would be lucky to receive $100 for it from a friend. People don't care to give you a decent price, especially the pawnshop. They give the scrap price for the gold. If the pawnshop owner doesn't like the design of your jewelry, they'll buy it to melt and recycle. In both cases, they want to make a profit. The further they talk you down, the larger their profit margin. So, you'll walk out of there with enough money for a hoagie to split with the family and be broke again. Hood bankruptcy is brutal. So, if pawnshops lowball us, why do we continue to sell our valuable physical assets to them for well below the asset's market price?

Simple.

Because of a term called liquidity.

How fast you can exchange an asset for cash without losing the market price determines the liquidity. In this case, if I'm trying to sell my gold necklace and can't find a buyer willing to pay the market price, the asset isn't liquid. That explains why there's so much jewelry at the pawnshop (because too many people failed to find the marketplace where buyers are willing to pay the market price for their assets.) So, the pawnshop owners buy our assets at extreme discounts guaranteed to make them a profit. The seller's experience occurred because they needed money and had physical assets that weren't liquid.

Every asset in the world has a market. But, as the owner of the asset, it's your responsibility to identify that market as an investor. There's a buyer out there willing to pay the market price for your gold necklace. This is the importance of understanding the market of an investment.

I'll give another example. A house isn't a liquid asset. When people need money and run out of things to sell, the house is next after falling behind on mortgage payments. Foreclosure is an exceedingly popular term and is like car repossession. The homeowner fails to make their monthly payments or other fees, and the lender takes the unpaid property.

In most cases, foreclosure occurs because people don't have money when they need it most. When people sell their houses under pressure, buyers hunt them like prey, trying to persuade them to sell their homes for less than the market value simply because they need money now. Buyers are hunting for what we call the four Ds: death, disaster, divorce, and debt. There's an endless amount of pressure and stress on the seller to liquidate the property in all those situations. But if the seller had an emergency fund in place, the risk of losing their property significantly decreases. Does it make sense now why risk management comes before investments? Having restricted access to cash could put you in a position to lose valuable assets. Don't be on the next episode of *Storage Wars* because you were buying assets with no market for them.

THE FACE OF INVESTMENTS

Physical assets require tender, loving care. I own plenty of physical assets, but I also accept the baggage that comes with them. I can't say the same about stocks, though. Investing in the stock market doesn't have the same risks as physical assets. I don't have to worry about someone walking off with my assets, because I manage my stocks through an online brokerage. This highly regulated platform is the middleman between investor transactions and a securities exchange.

Financial securities are stocks, bonds, and mutual funds.

Stocks are listed on a securities exchange where brokers handle the transactions. The security of your stock investments is how well you protect access to your brokerage account. It should be no different from how you treat your online bank account. Speaking of banks, in the same way they're FDIC-insured, brokers are insured by SIPC, terms that are truly worthless to know because the probability of a bank or broker going bankrupt is unlikely.

Stocks are known to be liquid assets. If I'm short on cash, I can go to my brokerage account and liquidate my stocks for cash. This is because the marketplace for stocks is easily accessible to everyone. You have to find someone to buy your jewelry or wait months to sell your house. Each stock has a metric called volume, which refers to the number of shares traded in a stock. It's common to see larger companies' volumes surpass millions in a day. This means you can more than likely sell your stocks at the market price. Now, you may see lower volumes in some companies and probably still be able to liquidate your shares at the market price. But it's not uncommon to have trouble liquidating shares in penny stocks at the market price. You'll also notice that most penny stocks have very low volumes compared to larger companies. Low volumes hint that it may be challenging to sell your shares.

The stock market has no barrier to entry like many other assets do. In real estate, it doesn't matter if you buy the nicest house at the end of the cul-de-sac or the most raggedy house in the city; the property will cost thousands. However, stocks have no barrier. When you search for a company on the stock market, the market price for one share appears. One share or stock can range from thousands to below $1, depending on the company.

What if you want to buy a share from a company with a market price of $1,000 per stock, but you only have $50?

Some brokers offer fractional shares, meaning you can buy $50 worth of stock in that company. In this case, you would own 5 percent of a share. This allows smaller investors to participate in the investment returns of some of their favorite companies, like Tesla and Amazon.

It's not uncommon to hold on to valuable collectible assets for long periods to allow the asset to appreciate, or increase, in value. That's how you receive a return on your investment, right? The best example is sports memorabilia. How much does a card of your favorite rookie this season cost? Let's assume you hold on to that rookie card for twenty years and that player is inducted into the Hall of Fame. How much do you think the card is worth compared to when you bought it? A lot! In the grand scheme, you bought an asset, held it for twenty years, and sold it.

In the stock market, companies pay investors cash dividends periodically, quarterly, semi-annually, or annually. Dividends are simply a passive stream of income. A company pays dividends to return a percentage of its profits to its long-term investors. The amount of dividends a company pays the investor per share is called the dividend yield. The yield is a percentage of how much a company pays per share in dividends. So, if you own a single $100 share of stock that has a dividend yield of 10 percent, this means you receive $10 annually in dividends for every share owned. Imagine how much passive income you could create if you continue to faithfully buy more shares.

I had a mentor that was very conservative about investing. He didn't touch his stock portfolio often because he was invested in some great companies that paid dividends. Besides his day job, which easily surpassed six figures, he received $150,000 in dividends annually. Before taxes, the man got approximately $12,500 per month in passive income from stock dividends. If that doesn't motivate you to create another passive income, I'm unsure what will.

The stock market is like an amusement park to most new participants. They put in a few dollars to hop on the rollercoaster and jump off the ride at the safest landing. Let me tell you, every bone in my body would be broken if that ride were real. I've ridden on carts with no wheels, sparks flying one hundred miles per hour downhill. Who doesn't love a rush? Then we go and tell our friends how much fun we had. We forget to mention the part about how we nearly died. That's because we fail to calculate risk before making an initial decision and manage risk throughout the process. Remember this rule of thumb: No one consistently beats the market. Let me explain.

The stock market has an index. This measures the entire stock market's performance. When you hear someone say, "the stock market is up" or "the stock market is down," they're referring to an index's performance. The most popular stock market indexes are the Dow Jones, S&P 500, and Nasdaq. Generally, the S&P 500 is the most popular. The S&P 500 stands for Standard & Poor's 500 companies of America. This index has 500 of America's largest companies, like Apple, Microsoft, Google, Walmart, and Starbucks. All those companies are combined into an index representing the entire stock market's performance. The S&P 500 is mainly chosen over other indexes like the famous Dow Jones because the Dow only chooses 30 companies to represent the whole stock market. Think about it—what would better represent the stock market: an index with the 30 strongest companies or a larger sample size of 500 of the most dominant companies in America?

The S&P 500 is the answer.

Nasdaq has more than 3,000 companies in its index. However, Nasdaq focuses on all the heavyweight tech companies.

The Dow Jones has been around since 1896. It was the first index to track stock activity. The average annual return from its inception to January 2019 is about 5 percent. The S&P 500's inception was in 1926, but the index didn't start tracking 500 companies until 1957. From the inception of the S&P to the end of 2022, the average annual return is approximately 10 percent. The average annual return for the S&P 500 holds true if we tracked from 1957 to the end of 2022 (Maverick 2023).

In context, if your returns are above the S&P 500, you beat the market that year. But listen to the greats. No one has consistently beaten the market every year by picking their stock portfolio. You don't have to miss out on the stock market gains (i.e., the largest 500 companies in one index). There are exchange-traded funds (ETFs) that can save your life. Those are generally passively managed assets that you can buy or sell like stocks in the market.

A good example is an index fund. You can buy ETFs on the stock market that tracks the S&P, Dow, or Nasdaq and pay dividends. I'm telling you that you can own one share that includes the performance of 500 of America's strongest companies. So, not only can you maximize your returns in the markets, but you can also start building another stream of income with dividend income.

COMPOUND INTEREST IS THE NAME OF THE GAME

Imagine a bill you save $200 for every month. At the end of the year, you'll have saved $2,400. That equates to $72,000 of your own cash in thirty years. Not that impressive over thirty years, right? When you include the magic of compound interest, which means accumulating interest and reinvesting those proceeds, you begin to put money to work. Let's say that at the end of every year you've decided to invest that $2,400 into an index fund. In this case, your index fund increases 10 percent annually from the increase in the price with a 4 percent annual dividend yield. Your balance at the end of thirty years will be near $769,000. This is the importance of why you should consistently invest and reinvest dividends. Your money made you nearly $700,000.

And guess what?

You didn't have to actively manage your account because you're invested in the strongest companies across America. What better way to leverage time as a retail investor?

Index funds are appreciated by a small population and don't receive the respect they deserve. Index funds are one of the most bulletproof ways to participate in the markets and take advantage of the performance of the strongest companies in America while you leverage time. Remember, time is our most valuable asset. Why do you think we all want passive income? To generate income while we spend time elsewhere. That time could be with family, building a business, serving your purpose, or creating another stream of income. But how do you leverage time if you continuously check the markets because the stocks you bought are volatile and high risk? My stock accounts generate dividends without me actively managing them. Property managers manage my real estate, so I receive calls maybe once a quarter and a paycheck every month on the fifteenth . I have a few other private passive incomes coming from elsewhere. The establishment of passive streams of income allows me to leverage time.

MY BOY REALLY DO INVEST

Let me rewind just a bit to tie everything together. Once you decide to pursue your version of success, build a budget that supports your goals. As you continue to earn and progress in life, you'll protect what you've earned by keeping an emergency fund and insuring your most valuable assets, including your limbs (health insurance). Next, to clear up your financial history, conscience, and voicemail, you'll get rid of debt. There's nothing cool about leaving debt on your books. Whatever crew says otherwise, they can't sit with us. Winners only! Once your life is stabilized, you're ready to make some financial investments to create passive income streams. Throughout the process, remember: "my boy really do invest (MBRDI)," which stands for mindset, budget, risk, management, debt, investments. You invest in yourself because you understand that you are your biggest investment. Once you get the hang of things, you'll work in systems to optimize time. Time is the most critical factor. I can't stress it enough. When you start working in systems and receive passive income, you maximize time. You'll just have to review the system you've created and read reports from your passive streams of income to make critical decisions. Are you ready to make some changes?

Don't wait. Remember, no one will take care of you the way you take care of yourself.

We compared a stock to a car. Explain the comparisons to the stock market.

Engine: ....

Trunk: ....

Tires: ....

Windshield: ....

Weather: ....

Similar car: ....

What are KPIs? Name two examples:

1. ....

2. ....

What's the difference between an undervalued stock and an overvalued stock?

....

....

Share two reasons individual stocks are risky.

1. ....

2. ....

What are the four ways to protect the value of physical assets?

1. ....

2. ....

3. ....

4. ....

Why do people usually sell their valuables to a pawn shop? (Hint: marketplace)

....

Circle *true* or *false*. Every asset in the world has a market.

What is one of the most bulletproof ways to participate in the stock market with minimum knowledge and take advantage of the performance of the strongest companies in America?

....

PART VI

THE GRAND
SCHEME

A HOME WITH A FENCE

We begin our financial journey at various levels because of inheritance, resources, or both. The home and fence are symbolic of your financial journey. A fence is a protection mechanism commonly used as the first line of defense for the home. The fence is your emergency fund. It protects your financial well-being and everything you've worked to acquire. It's important to keep your fence in good shape, or it's useless, right?

The outside of your home normally reflects your social status, and the inside reflects your quality of life. The home is symbolic of an investment vehicle. You begin with what you have and continue to make contributions, sort of like home improvements. Each room is a different investment. Don't expect to upgrade every room in the first year. Eventually, your home or investment vehicle will give you a return on investment.

Let's not forget the tree. Some of us have a forest! The tree is symbolic of the things you buy that mean nothing or have no long-term economic value. Keep the tree under control. The leaves from the tree can clog your gutters, fall onto your home, or block your view.

Clothes:	$3,500
Shoes:	$1,500
Electronics:	$4,000
	$9,000

Investment:
$1,000

Emergency Fund:
$500

Clothes we buy are made to be worn and normally resell for a fraction of the retail price. Therefore, expensive clothes are a notable example of something we buy with no long-term economic value.

As time passes, you should continue upgrading your home. A fence upgrade symbolizes a greater line of defense or better stability with an emergency fund.

For example, let's say your old fence represents a $500 emergency fund, or half of a month's rent. The new fence represents $3,000, or three-months' worth of rent in the example below. The fence becomes sturdier and more difficult to penetrate for unwelcome visitors, or what we know as unexpected expenses.

Periodically, you'll want to renovate sections of your home. Renovations require out-of-pocket money. The renovations symbolize adding money to your initial investment. It takes money to make money. The more money you consistently put into your investment, the greater the return on investment.

For example, you might renovate your dividend stocks. Let's say you owned 100 shares of stock at $10 each (for a total cost of $1,000) and saw a return of 10 percent each year. With this initial investment, you would receive $100 in dividends each year for owning 100 shares of stock. Each time you receive a paycheck from work, you continue adding to your investment, buying more shares. Let's say you accumulate 200 shares at $10 each (for a total cost of $2,000) and saw a return of 10 perfect each year. After adding more money to your investment, you would receive $200 in dividends each year for owning 200 shares.

It's obvious in this image that the trees are under control and trimmed, which is symbolic of unnecessary spending being reduced and properly managed.

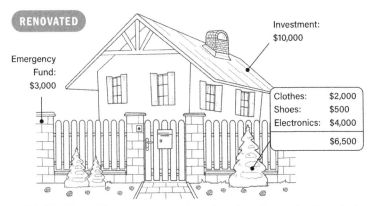

RENOVATED

Investment:
$10,000

Emergency
Fund:
$3,000

Clothes:	$2,000
Shoes:	$500
Electronics:	$4,000
	$6,500

Don't feel bad for deciding to reduce your closet. Some items in your closet have bad energy. This includes unwanted memories that could be sad, depressing, or don't define you anymore.

Now, there are two different homes below. We have Home A and Home B. The difference between the two is how focused you are with a larger amount of money in your pocket. As you increase your buying power, the temptation of "I deserve to treat myself" will rush in like never before. The things you could never afford will be the first on your radar—the cars, the clothes, the nice shoes. You must stay focused, though. It's easier said than done.

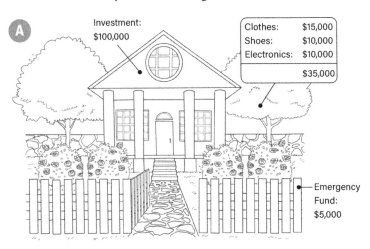

A

Investment:
$100,000

Clothes:	$15,000
Shoes:	$10,000
Electronics:	$10,000
	$35,000

Emergency
Fund:
$5,000

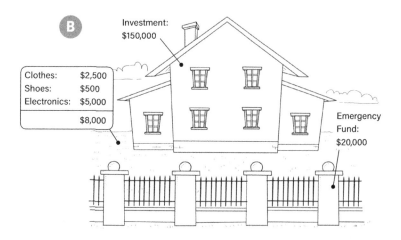

Remember, it takes money to make money. The more you invest, the more possible it will be to get a return on investment. It's your decision. Which home will you choose to build?

The truth is that there's more to life than wrapping your mind around financial concepts and studying the stock market. Don't allow aggressive marketers on social media to make you feel like you're missing out on the greatest thing since sliced bread. Your world doesn't have to revolve around who has the most money. You'll never find happiness chasing the wind because you'll never catch it. When money becomes your motive, you'll do slimy things to honest people. Let me just say that there's no honor among thieves. The only thing mandatory for you is to manage the money in your possession. Take care of business and enjoy your time on this Earth with the people you love most.

BOTTOM LINE

The purpose of creating this book is to ensure you're a critical thinker in your household. I'm not encouraging you to buy individual stocks or pressuring you to start a business. I'm giving you a sharp financial ax to chop down every problematic tree in your way. The roots of some of your problematic trees may be deeper and larger than other trees you came across in the past, requiring help from someone more well-equipped. Find professional help. Get rid of all your problematic trees to focus on planting seeds of generational wealth.

Never forget this: You are your greatest investment!

What are the most important takeaways from each section? Be detailed because the more you can analyze the information, the better you can apply it to your life.

Mindset:

Budget:

Risk Management:

Debt:

Investments:

List a few of your goals after reading this book.

1. ....

2. ....

3. ....

4. ....

5. ....

How can you fund some of the goals in your budget?

....

....

....

....

....

....

ABOUT THE AUTHOR

"How do I become a financial critical thinker?"

It has been Bergen's goal from the beginning to solve this very simple yet complex question. Bergen has self-studied money management for a decade, since he was living in poverty. He documented his journey from the inner city to the military and on to managing the financial planning of billions of dollars of operating expenses for over 3,000 logistic assets in private equity.

Bergen has spent the last decade formalizing a clear-cut financial process with five simple steps for anyone to create financial stability and build wealth while achieving their goals. This has led him to build the financial literacy platform Walk With Me to help millions of people along their journey of elevation. Bergen's goal is to meet you where you are in life at this moment and transform you into the chief financial officer and financial critical thinker in your household. Let's walk.

To learn more about the author, please visit
myfinancialwalk.com

Instagram: *@bergenbrownjr*

Facebook: *Bergen Brown*

REFERENCES

Betterton, Rebecca. 2023. "Average auto loan payments: What to expect in 2023." Bankrate. April 26, 2023. *https://www. bankrate.com/loans/auto-loans/average-monthly-car-payment/*

Brooks, Khristopher J. 2023. "Most Americans say they can't cover a $1,000 emergency cost." CBS News. January 25, 2023. *https://www.yahoo.com/now/most-americans-cant-cover-1-230200350.html*

Everytown Research & Policy. 2022. "A Nation of Survivors: The Toll of Gun Violence in America." *https://everytownresearch.org/report/a-nation-of-survivors-the-toll-of-gun-violence-in-america/*

Gillett, Rachel. 2015. "How Walt Disney, Oprah Winfrey, and 19 Other Successful People Rebounded After Getting Fired." Inc. October 7, 2015. *https://www.inc.com/business-insider/21-successful-people-who-rebounded-after-getting-fired.html*

Healthcare.gov. 2019. "Health Coverage Protects You from High Medical Costs." *www.healthcare.gov/why-coverage-is-important/protection-from-high-medical-costs/*

LinkedIn. 2016. "New Survey Reveals 85% of All Jobs are Filled Via Networking." *https://www.linkedin.com/pulse/new-survey-reveals-85-all-jobs-filled-via-networking-lou-adler/*

Lurie, Stephen. 2019. "There's No Such Thing as a Dangerous Neighborhood." February 25, 2019. Bloomberg. *https://www.bloomberg.com/tosv2.html?vid=&uuid=85f6b4e8-0d7 3-11ec-bf4e-66625062624f&url=L25ld3MvYXJ0aWNsZX- MvMjAxOS0wMi0yNS9iZXlvbmQtYnJva2VuLXdpbmRvwd- 3Mtd2hhdC1yZWFsbHktZHJpdmVzLXVyYmFuL- WNyaW1l*

Maverick, J.B.. 2023. "S&P 500 Average Return." Investopedia. February 15, 2023. https://www.investopedia.com/ask/answers/042415/what-average-annual-return-sp-500.asp

Papachristos, Andrew V., Christopher Wildeman, and Elizabeth Roberto. "Tragic, but Not Random: The Social Contagion of Nonfatal Gunshot Injuries." *Social Science & Medicine* 125 (2015):139–150, https://doi.org/10.1016/j.socscimed.2014.01.056

Stolba, Stephen. 2021. "Average U.S. Consumer Debt Reaches New Record in 2020." Experian. June 4, 2021. *www.experian.com/blogs/ask-experian/research/consumer-debt-study/*

Semega, Jessica, Melissa Kollar, Emily A. Shrider, and John F. Creamer. 2021. "Income and Poverty in the United States: 2019." U.S. Government Publishing Office. Last modified September 2021. *www.census.gov/content/dam/Census/library/publications/2020/demo/p60-270.pdf*

Woods, Laura. 2020. "13 Ludicrous Company Lawsuits in the Last Decade." Yahoo! Sports. August 4, 2020. *www.sports.yahoo.com/crazy-lawsuits-ridiculous-payouts-090000559.html*

Zillow. 2019. "What Is the Average Time to Sell a House?." November 26, 2019. *www.zillow.com/sellers-guide/average-time-to-sell-a-house/*

Made in the USA
Middletown, DE
27 June 2023

33972076R00066